P9-DHO-433

IMAGES
of America

CHARLESTOWN

The Boston and Lynn horsecar traveled along Chelsea Street in Charlestown. In the rear are the lower officers' houses in the Charlestown Navy Yard.

IMAGES
of America

CHARLESTOWN

Anthony Mitchell Sammarco

ARCADIA

First published 1996
Copyright © Anthony Mitchell Sammarco, 1996

ISBN 0-7524-0469-5

Published by Arcadia Publishing,
an imprint of the Chalford Publishing Corporation
One Washington Center, Dover, New Hampshire 03820
Printed in Great Britain

Boys are pushing a popcorn cart up Cordis Street in 1954. With the aroma of freshly popped corn and hot oil in the air, these popcorn carts provided a popular street food in Boston a few decades ago.

Contents

Introduction

On January 1, 1874, the City of Charlestown, Massachusetts, was officially annexed to the City of Boston. A city since its incorporation in 1847, Charlestown became part of a thriving metropolis composed of once-independent towns that supported the burgeoning population and expansion of Boston.

Settled in 1628, Charlestown was originally known as "Mishawum" by the Native Americans. Wonohaquaham (known to the Puritans as Sagamore John), a member of the Pawtucket tribe, sold the lands to the English. Originally, Charlestown encompassed a much larger land area than it does today, as it included Somerville, Malden, Everett, Woburn, Stoneham, and Burlington, as well as parts of Medford, Cambridge, Arlington, and Reading. Within a few years, Charlestown—named in honor of King Charles I—had become a bustling town that attracted new settlers from England.

The fierce Revolutionary War battle that took place on Breed's Hill in Charlestown on June 17, 1775—an event that posterity has recorded as the Battle of Bunker Hill—represents the most widely known aspect of Charlestown's history. At that critical juncture in the forging of America's independence, U.S. troops under the direction of Colonel Prescott, General Putnam, and Major Brooks defended their land against the British. General Putnam's dictum that day—"Don't fire until you see the whites of their eyes"—has become famous, but the stalwart American troops were forced to retreat from their position in the end. The British troops took further devastating and decisive action after the battle when they burned the town to the ground.

Though most Americans associate Charlestown with the Battle of Bunker Hill, the city actually has a long and rich history outside of that event. John

Harvard (1607–1638) was admitted in 1637 as a freeman to Charlestown, where he was a "sometime minister of God's Word." Though he died the following year, his bequest of half of his estate and his entire library to the new college in Cambridge led to that famous school being named in his honor. Harvard's bequest ensured the future of the college at "Newtowne," now Cambridge.

After the Revolution, Charlestown was slowly rebuilt with Market Square (later City Square) as the center of town government. Numerous unique forms of transportation developed in order to maintain accessibility to Boston, including the "penny ferry" in the seventeenth century, the horse-drawn omnibus in the early nineteenth century, and the Elevated Railway in the twentieth century. From the Charlestown Navy Yard, such famous ships as the *Constitution* (or "Old Ironsides") were launched, and the city's industrial concerns were varied and significant. The Stickney and Poor Spice Company, the Schrafft and Cowdrey candy companies, the Diamond Match Company, and the Davidson Syringe Company were all based in Charlestown, and from the latter two firms came two firsts in American history: wooden matches and rubber syringes. Both inventions were patented and distributed worldwide.

Today, Charlestown is a neighborhood of the City of Boston. Accessible by the Charlestown Bridge, which connects the North End and City Square, the town is known for its restored early nineteenth-century houses, the redeveloped Navy Yard, gas lamps, and the Bunker Hill Monument. An independent city from 1847 to 1874, with a fascinating industrial base in the nineteenth century, Charlestown has a rich and fascinating history, much of which is brought to life in the photographs that follow.

One
City of Charlestown

Seen from the Copp's Hill Burial Ground in Boston's North End, this view of Charlestown was drawn by John Warner Barber for his 1839 book, *Historical Collections of Massachusetts*. The unfinished Bunker Hill Monument rises on Breed's Hill and the Charlestown Navy Yard is on the far right.

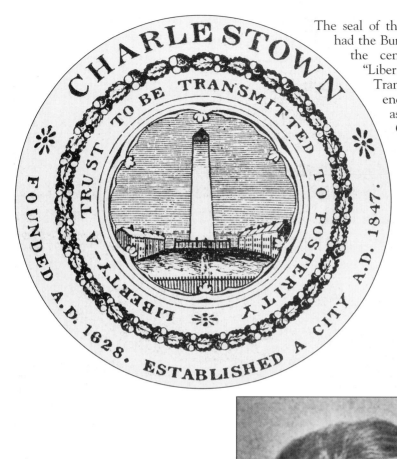

The seal of the City of Charlestown had the Bunker Hill Monument in the center with the motto "Liberty—A Trust to Be Transmitted To Posterity" encircling it. Established as a city in 1847, Charlestown would later be annexed to the City of Boston in 1874.

Henry Fairbanks (1808–1854) was a member of the Charlestown Common Council, serving as president between 1849 and 1853. He was also a member and the first president of the erudite Charlestown Lyceum.

Charlestown City Hall was built in "City Square," the junction of Warren Street, Charles River (now Rutherford) Avenue, and Chelsea Street. An impressive French Second Empire building with a mansard roof and center dome, it served as city offices until 1874. The enclosed park and fountain in the foreground were laid out prior to the Civil War when the area was known as Market Square (it was renamed City Square in 1847).

James Dana (1811–1890) was mayor of Charlestown between 1858 and 1861. A graduate of Harvard College and Yale Law School, Dana was an attorney that had "a taste for politics and always took a great interest in public matters." During Dana's term as mayor, a public library was established for residents.

Horace G. Hutchins (1811–1877) was mayor of Charlestown in 1861. An attorney with the Boston law firm of Hutchins and Willey, he "won for himself a splendid reputation as a presiding officer and also as a man of executive ability."

Phineas Jones Stone (1810–1897) was mayor of Charlestown between 1862 and 1864. Serving as mayor during the Civil War, he raised and formed several companies of soldiers that served in the Union Army.

William H. Kent (1823–1889) was mayor of Charlestown between 1870 and 1872. Associated with the lumber industry for many years, he became president of the Mill Owner's Fire Insurance Company while serving as mayor.

Jonathan Stone (1823–1899) was mayor of Charlestown in 1873 and 1874. Charlestown was annexed to the city of Boston on January 1, 1874, the same day that West Roxbury and Brighton became parts of the city.

Shortly after Charlestown was annexed to Boston, this bird's-eye view of the town was taken from the Bunker Hill Monument looking west. The school in the right foreground is the Charlestown High School, which was built in 1870 on Monument Square. On the upper right is the Saint Francis de Sales Church on Bunker Hill Street.

Looking to the east from the Bunker Hill Monument, the spire of Saint Catherine's Church can be seen on the far left. The Mystic River divides Chelsea and Everett from Charlestown; row houses were built closely together on the streets between the monument and Bunker Hill Street, including Lexington, Jackson, Edgeworth, and Hunter Streets, and Nearen Row.

The district post office was located at 23 Main Street on the first floor of the Charlestown Gas Company building. Abram E. Cutter stands in the center wearing a light-colored jacket with others in front of the post office entrance in 1889. (Courtesy of the Reverend Wolcott Cutler Collection, Charlestown Branch, Boston Public Library, hereinafter referred to as the BPL.)

Edward F. Barker was appointed superintendent of the Charlestown Post Office in January 1876.

The Charlestown Cadets, Company A, 5th Infantry, MVM were uniformed and officered in 1858 as successors to the Charlestown Militia. Captain Willis Whittemore Stover is seated in the first row, with First Lieutenant William S. Tolman and Second Lieutenant Rowland W. Bray on either side of him.

John E. Phipps was one of the organizers of the Charlestown Cadets, originally a local drill club. Appointed captain of the Cadets in 1874, he was chief marshal of two Bunker Hill Day parades, which were held annually on the 17th of June.

The Charlestown City Guard, Company D, 4th Regiment, Light Infantry succeeded the Company B, Charlestown Light Infantry, in 1846. Captain Francis Meredith Jr. is seated in the center of the first row with First Lieutenant Fred McDonald and Second Lieutenant Henry Y. Gilson seated on either side.

Abraham Edmands Cutter was a partner in the bookstore of McKim and Cutter, which opened in Charlestown in 1852. Elected in 1857 to the school board of Charlestown, Cutter was always "identified with, and interested in, the various local charities and institutions of the city."

The Poorhouse at Charlestown was an almshouse that had "a homelike character which the larger institution lacks." The "worthy poor" (considered to be the aged, sick, and the physically and mentally disabled) and the "unworthy poor" (all the rest) found refuge from their troubles here.

Old couples at the Charlestown Poorhouse pose in their rocking chairs on the front porch in 1893. It was said that "special provision is made for the comfort of the aged and infirm, and the treatment of the sick is by the most improved methods."

Benjamin Phipps (1797–1878) was a member of the family that Phipps Street was named for. As a founder and first treasurer of the Winchester Home for Aged Couples, he was a well-respected member of the community.

The entrance to the Phipps Street burial ground is seen from Lawrence Street. A gas street lamp projects from the building on the left, and towering elm trees arch gracefully over this ancient cemetery, which is being restored through the City of Boston's Historic Burying Ground Initiative. (Courtesy of the BPL.)

The obelisk erected to the memory of John Harvard (1607–1638) rises 15 feet from the highest point in the Phipps Street burial ground. Dedicated on September 26, 1828, "by the graduates of the university at Cambridge, in honor of its founder, who died at Charlestown," the obelisk commemorates the Puritan minister who left one half of his estate to the new college in Cambridge, which has borne his name in grateful memory ever since.

The Bunker Hill Cemetery is on Bunker Hill Street, between Elm and Polk Streets, and was opened in 1803. A pathway divides family lots that were embellished in the nineteenth century with cast-iron urns and, in some cases, decorative railings. (Courtesy of the BPL.)

Two
Churches

The First Parish Church in Charlestown was just off City Square. An impressive Romanesque Revival brick church, it was photographed on June 17, 1878. (Courtesy of the First Parish Church in Charlestown, hereinafter referred to as the First Parish Church.)

The Charlestown Meeting House was an impressive church with a steeple designed by the noted architect Charles Bulfinch. With a clock below the belfry, its soaring spire could be distinctly seen from the North End of Boston.

The First Congregational Church was built in 1833. A simple but impressive Greek Revival church, it had a classical belfry of Ionic columns supporting a gilded dome.

FIRST CONGREGATIONAL CHURCH,
BUILT 1833.

Reverend George E. Ellis, third pastor of the Harvard Unitarian Church in Charlestown, served as a professor of Systematic Theology at the Harvard Divinity School and was president of the Massachusetts Historical Society. An accomplished and prolific writer, he was the author of a number of chapters in Justin Winsor's *Memorial History of Boston*.

Reverend Jedediah Morse (1761–1826) was minister of the Charlestown Meeting House and the author of the first geography book published in the United States. A graduate of Yale, his books on geography included *Geography Made Easy* (1784), *The American Geography* (1789), and *The American Gazetteer* (1797). His portrait was painted—with his geographies and a book of his sermons on a shelf behind him—by his son Samuel F.B. Morse, c. 1810. (Courtesy of the Yale University Art Gallery.)

Elizabeth Ann Breese Morse (c. 1765–1828) was the quintessential minister's wife in the late eighteenth century. Elizabeth was the daughter of Samuel Breese (the founder of Shrewsbury, New Jersey) and the granddaughter of Samuel Finley (a president of Princeton), and was a well-educated and forthright woman in her own right. The luminous quality of her portrait shows the obvious talent of her son Samuel. (Courtesy of the Yale University Art Gallery.)

The Harvard Unitarian Church was at the corner of Main and Green Streets, the present site of the Charlestown Branch, Boston Public Library. Built in 1817 on the site of the former Indian Chief Hotel, the church received a spire in 1851. (Courtesy of the BPL.)

The Harvard Chapel was established by Reverend George E. Ellis on Edgeworth Street to minister to the religious needs of the less fortunate citizens of Charlestown. A small wood-framed chapel, it was reorganized in 1871 by Reverend Charles F. Barnard as the Independent Church of Charlestown. (Courtesy of the BPL.)

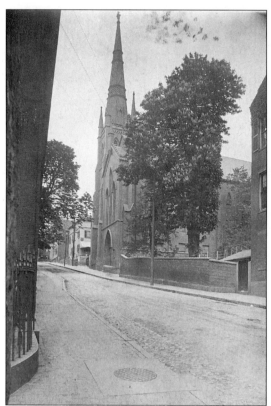

The Winthrop Church was built on Green Street, just up the hill from Main Street. A Gothic Revival church, it is today the First Church in Charlestown. (Courtesy of the First Parish Church.)

Looking down the hill from High Street, the Winthrop Church was built on the site of the garden of Rhodes Greene Lockwood. The Davidson-Lockwood Mansion was later to become the headquarters of the Abraham Lincoln Post, Grand Army of the Republic, seen on the left. (Courtesy of the First Parish Church.)

The Trinity Methodist Church was built in 1867 on the site of an earlier church destroyed by fire. Built on High Street, near Green Street, it was "said to have been made more nearly uninflammable than any other public building ever erected in Charlestown until modern times." (Courtesy of the BPL.)

The choir of the First Church in Charlestown poses on Easter Sunday in 1929. (Courtesy of the First Parish Church.)

Saint Mary's Church was the first Roman Catholic Church built in Charlestown. Originally on Charles River Avenue (now Rutherford Avenue), it was the second church opened for Catholics in the area, the first being the Cathedral of the Holy Cross on Franklin Street in Boston. This church, a simple Greek Revival structure with unusual towers flanking the nave, was dedicated in 1829 and used until 1887, when the present Saint Mary's Church on Warren Street was built.

Reverend John W. McMahon was pastor of Saint Mary's Church during its centennial anniversary in 1928. A native of Charlestown, he served the parish for over fifty years and his "principal labor has been the erection of a larger church in place of the old chapel on what is now Rutherford Avenue."

The present Saint Mary's Church was built in 1887 on Warren Street between Soley and Winthrop Streets. An impressive Gothic-style church of Rockport granite and brick trimmings, it was designed by Patrick C. Keeley. The cornerstone was laid by Reverend McMahon on October 29, 1887, and the church was dedicated in 1892.

Members of the Boys' Choir of Saint Mary's Church pose before the High Altar in 1901. (Courtesy of the BPL.)

Saint Mary's Convent was a former townhouse on Monument Square that faced the Bunker Hill Monument.

Mary McCarthy and Ray Daignault were married at Saint Mary's Church on August 10, 1949. The couple pose outside the church on Soley Street with their proud mothers on either side.

The Catholic Literary Union served all parishioners of Charlestown's three Catholic parishes: Saint Mary's, Saint Francis de Sales, and Saint Catherine's.

Saint Francis de Sales Church was dedicated on June 17, 1862. Built on Bunker Hill Street, its blue stone "Roman-Celtic" style was designed by Patrick C. Keeley, the foremost Catholic architect in the United States and the architect of numerous churches in the Archdiocese of Boston. The church "is supposed to have been modeled after some of the notable specimens of ancient chapels in Ireland before the tenth century."

Reverend Mark C. Driscoll was appointed pastor of Saint Francis de Sales Church in 1928. Father Driscoll had been ordained a priest in Rome, after having studied at the North American College. It was said that during Father Driscoll's editorship of *The Pilot*, a Catholic newspaper, that "the publication grew rapidly, becoming one of the foremost and strongest Diocesan journals in the country."

Three

Schools, the Library, and Clubs

These young schoolgirls were enrolled in "domestic science," a course offered in the Boston Public School that stressed sewing, cooking, and associated "sciences." Posing in the kitchen of the Harvard School, they wore mop caps and aprons while learning of the art of making breads and cakes.

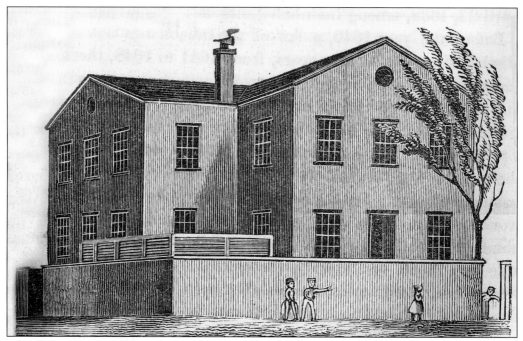

The Warren Schoolhouse was built in 1840 and was named for Dr. Joseph Warren (1741–1775), who was killed during the Battle of Bunker Hill.

Warren School
Charlestown, Mass.

The second structure of the Warren School was built in 1857 on Summer Street. Schoolchildren are shown here posing in the school yard in 1905.

The Harvard School was built in 1871 on Devens Street. It was named for Reverend John Harvard, the minister who settled on Town Hill in 1637 and bequeathed half his estate and his entire library of 320 books to the new college in "Newtowne."

Students of the Harvard School pose for their class portrait in 1884.

The Frothingham School was an impressive brick and granite school that was named in 1876 for Richard Frothingham (1812–1879), a member of the Massachusetts House of Representatives and the town historian of Charlestown.

Richard Frothingham was mayor of Charlestown from 1851 to 1853 and delivered the address in 1869 at the dedication of the Charlestown City Hall. His *History of Charlestown* chronicled the early history of the town and he later counted among his writings the *History of the Siege of Boston* and *The Rise of the Republic of the United States*.

Young girls who were pupils of the Frothingham School had sewing classes to augment their educational courses. Mary Tileston Hemenway was a member of the Boston School Committee with a large personal fortune at her disposal, and she began the introduction of domestic sciences to the school system. In association with fellow school committee member Emily Fifield, Hemenway established courses that would prepare non-college bound girls for jobs once they graduated.

Kindergartners at the Nahim Chapin School in 1938–39 include, from left to right: (front row) Ellen Galvin, Anne Hartigan, Barbara Cox, Mary Terrell, Mary Murphy, James Fitzgibbons, Marian Houlahan, Elizabeth Randall, Richard Doherty, Donalda Kirk, Robert Harrington, and Kathleen Harrington; (middle row) Jean Gross, Ruth Sullivan, Pasquale Franzosa, Gerald Hurley, John Harrington, Arthur Crotty, Irene Plunkett, and Joseph Griffin; (back row) James Blute, John Regan, Joan Foley, Edward Fitzgerald, Helen Doherty, Paul Kelly, Arthur Prince, Joseph Mc Carthy, Dorothy Foley, Anne Kelley, Patricia Carroll, Edward Foley, Elizabeth Kerley, and Herbert La Freniere. (Courtesy of the BPL.)

The Charlestown High School was built in 1870 on Monument Square. An impressive Italianate school with a mansard roof, it had a clock above a dormer window that could be seen from all parts of Monument Square. (Courtesy of the BPL.)

Company D of the Charlestown High School Cadets poses on the lawn surrounding the Bunker Hill Monument in 1891. Captain Bill Coates, First Lieutenant Fred Lincoln, and Second Lieutenant Frank Sanderson stand in front of company members Lawrence Sager, Ted Berry, Ed Scott, Bill Robbins, Percy Sawyer, Phil Shaw, Jean Stowell, Charles Smith, George Chandler, Ted Fitzgerald, Arthur Towne, George Lord, Teddy Ayer, Walter Howe, Frank Curtis, Heine Thomforde, Arnie Stewart, and Guy Greene. (Courtesy of the BPL.)

A domestic arts teacher stands before her students, who are preparing food over burners in the Charlestown High School. With long aprons covering their dresses and caps over their hair, these girls learned various recipes that could be tried out at home.

Another course in the domestic arts was sewing, in which girls would sew the dress that was worn at graduation. On a trestle table, some girls are drawing on paper patterns that would be used to cut out cloth while others measure their fellow students. Notice the hats on the pegs behind the girls.

A new Charlestown High School was built on the site of the old school. Built of granite with Doric pilasters supporting a cornice inscribed "MDCCCXLIII (1848) Charlestown High School MDCCCVII (1907)," it served as the local high school until recently, when it was rehabilitated by Graham Gund Associates as luxury condominiums.

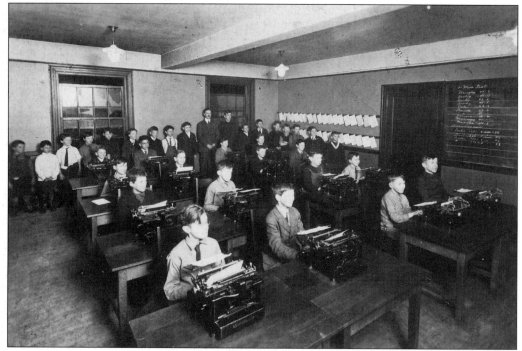

Students in a touch typewriting class learn how to type rather than how to perfect their handwriting. (Courtesy of the BPL.)

The Opportunity Club Orchestra performs in 1912 at the Charlestown High School. There were over one hundred Opportunity Clubs in Boston, all free to Boston residents, with a combined weekly attendance of twelve thousand people.

Girls and young women would meet in the evening to learn to sew and crochet during the weekly meetings of the Opportunity Club.

Saint Mary's School was a Catholic school for those who preferred a religious education for their children.

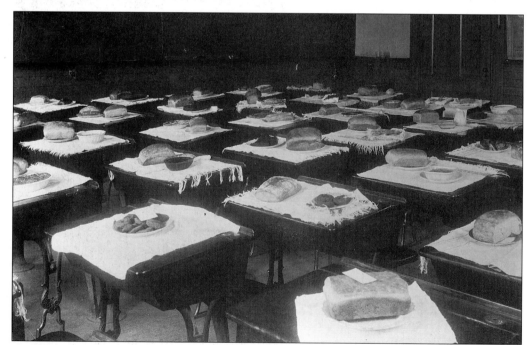

On the evening of parent-teacher meetings, a bread, cake, or sweet prepared by a student enrolled in cooking classes at the Charlestown High School was placed on her desk for sampling by her parents. Beware of the girl who couldn't *boil water*!

The Charlestown Branch, Boston Public Library, was originally on Monument Square. Today, this building is the Bunker Hill Museum. (Courtesy of the BPL.)

Two young patrons of the Charlestown Branch Library wait patiently for the doors to open at 1 pm . (Courtesy of the BPL.)

A gym class at the Charlestown Young Men's Christian Association (YMCA) poses with their trainer (on the left with a beard) when the "Y" was at the corner of Union and Lawrence Streets. (Courtesy of the BPL.)

The Saint Mary's Women's Club was located in an impressive townhouse on Monument Square. Here, literary evenings, lectures, and fund-raisers were held to benefit the parish.

Members of the Abraham Lincoln Post 11, Grand Army of the Republic (GAR), pose on Cordis Street on June 17, 1886. (Courtesy of the BPL.)

On June 17, 1905, marching members of the Joseph Warren Commandery, Knights Templar, are garbed in feathered hats, satin-lined capes, and swords as they march in the Bunker Hill Day parade.

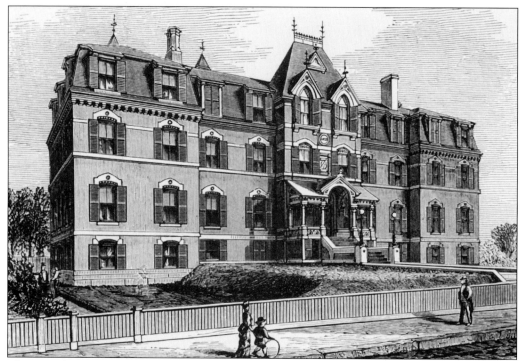

The Winchester Home for Aged Women was founded in 1865 through the generosity of Mrs. Nancy Winchester of Charlestown. An advertisement circulated shortly after it was founded said that the home "is maintained exclusively for people who have lived in Charlestown for ten years previous to application for admission."

Residents of the Winchester Home for Aged Women pose in costume in the 1920s. (Courtesy of the BPL.)

46

Four
Public Safety

Firemen of the Bunker Hill Engine Company pose outside their firehouse, which was on Main Street just below Cambridge Street. (Courtesy of the BPL.)

The Franklin Engine Company was a simple brick firehouse at the corner of Bunker Hill and Tufts Streets. (Courtesy of the BPL.)

Firemen of the Hancock Hose and Massachusetts Hook and Ladder Companies pose in 1885 outside their firehouse on Main Street. (Courtesy of the BPL.)

District Fire Chief Charles H. Pope (on the left) and his driver pose in a carriage on Winthrop Street in 1897. (Courtesy of the BPL.)

Charles H. Pope became a fireman at the age of twenty-three and it was said that "every mishap simply increased his courage and daring, and he always returned from each serious injury with even greater ardor than before. In 1887, his eyes were burned at a fire on the steamer *Venetian*. Two months later a kerosene stove exploded in his hands, wounding him in nearly every part of his body." Despite all this, he served with pride, albeit *wounded* pride!

Thomas W. Conway was initially with Ladder Number One before becoming captain of Ladder Company 12. In 1888, he was transferred as captain to Ladder Company 15.

Martin V. Kimball was captain of Engine Company 32. A veteran of the Civil War, he served in various firehouses until being promoted to captain in 1884.

This Boston fire boat was docked in Charlestown and was used to fight fires on wharves and ships docked in Boston. On the left, just behind the building, is the bridge connecting Boston's North End to City Square in Charlestown.

Boston fire boats used sea water to battle fires on the wharves and docks, as seen in this photograph of 1912.

Seth Low was captain of the Boston fire boat *William M. Flanders*. He was not only a member of the Veteran Firemen's Association, but the Royal Arcanum and the Charlestown Club.

Fire boat, Engine 31, was a more compact boat used to fight harbor fires.

Edward Gaskin was captain of Police Station 14 at the turn of the century. Appointed to the police force in 1874, he was promoted through the ranks until he became "the popular captain of Station 14."

Sullivan A. Johnston was appointed to the police department in 1868 and was promoted to sergeant in 1878. "Sergeant Johnston was never late for roll call since he became a member of the force, except when excused; he never received a reprimand from his superior officers; was never absent from duty a day but what he has made up by overtime."

Martin L. White was captain of Police Station 15 at the turn of the century.

Jeremiah McCarthy was a volunteer with the Bunker Hill Engine Company and later a member of the Washington Hose Company. He was the first treasurer of the Charlestown Volunteer Firemen's Association, and later served as a representative in the Massachusetts House of Representatives.

Five
The Navy Yard

The parade grounds of the Charlestown Navy Yard were in front of the marine barracks (in the center). On the right is the vegetable garden, and the Commandant's House can be seen through the trees on the left.

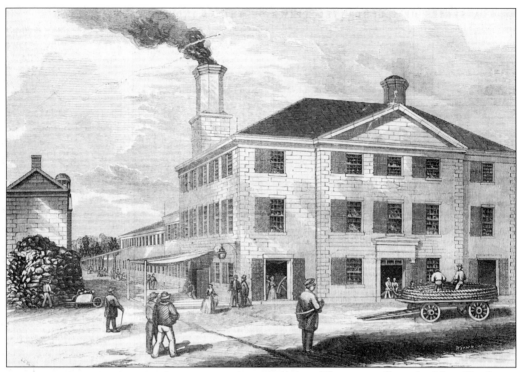

The ropewalk at the Navy Yard was housed in a granite building that had a long wing in the rear where one walked the rope until it was twisted, or furled. Two men here wind thick hemp rope on a cart that would be used on ships. Hemp, an Asiatic plant that has a tough fiber, was used to make sailcloth as well as rope.

William Austin (1778–1841) was the first commissioned chaplain in the United States Navy; he was appointed chaplain at the Charlestown Navy Yard in 1799. A graduate of Harvard College, he was also a well-known author whose books included *Peter Rugg, the Missing Man*, and *Letters from London*. So evocative were his writings that he was called "The Precursor of Hawthorne."

Entrance to the Navy Yard was gained by passing through a guard post on Chelsea Street. Here guards stand at order at the gates in 1890 while civilians stand to the left of the guard post on Chelsea Street.

The U.S. *Constitution* is the oldest commissioned ship in the United States Navy. Launched in 1797, "Old Ironsides" is a major attraction in Boston that is visited by thousands annually. Serving with great éclat in the War of 1812, the *Constitution* was saved from destruction and an ignoble end by the poem of Oliver Wendell Holmes.

The view of the Navy Yard from Chelsea Street in 1825 showed the Commandant's House in the center, with an alley of poplar trees lining the walk to the front door. Bunker Hill (actually Breed's Hill) rises on the left and the marine barracks and the Mystic River can be seen on the right.

The Commandant's House at the Navy Yard is an impressive double-swell bay facade of red brick. In this 1899 photograph, two little girls pose outside the fence separating the parade ground from the street.

This view looking southeast from the Bunker Hill Monument in 1876 shows the Navy Yard along the waterfront and the warship *Ohio* at dock. Across the harbor is East Boston, which was developed by the East Boston Company in the 1830s.

The Gun Park at the Navy Yard was photographed in 1880 with hundreds of cannons lining the ground in front of the Commandant's House (on the left) and the barracks.

"Lover's Walk" was a wood plank sidewalk that stretched alongside the barracks (on the left). Tree-lined Lover's Walk was a place where both officers and sailors could court, albeit in full view of all.

Sitting before a huge pile of cannon balls in 1892 are, from left to right, Sydney K. Clapp, Ridgeway Holbrook, and Frank L. Clapp.

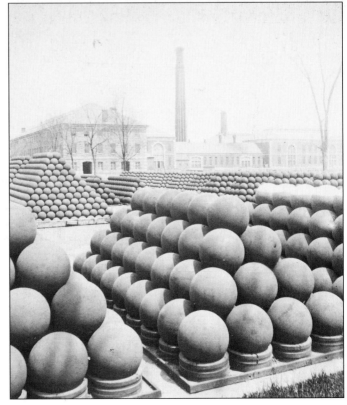

These cannons were neatly piled in what was referred to as the "Shot Park," an area in front of the Steam Engineering Building and the Joiner Shop. The chimney of the shop rose to a height of 236 feet.

In the Mystic Channel of the Mystic River were, from right to left: the schooner *George V. Jordan*, the barkentine *Altona*, the barkentine *Rachel S. Emery*, the bark *Auburndale*, and two unknown schooners that were loading lumber. By the 1890s, when this photograph was taken, the area was a bustling center of imports and immigrants.

In this 1908 photograph of the Boston Navy Yard, the Hoosic Terminal can be seen in the rear with ships at dock in the foreground.

Dry docks at the Navy Yard allowed ships to be repaired and painted. The ships would be floated into the dry docks, and the water then drained, allowing easy access to the hull.

A 729-foot dry dock for steam ships was built in the early twentieth century for the vastly enlarged ships of the U.S. Navy.

The cruiser *Maryland* was the first ship to be serviced in the new dry dock at the Navy Yard. An armored cruiser, the *Maryland* was fitted with armor belts of 18-inch thickness and would normally carry eight hundred men during a cruise.

The cruiser *Tennessee* and the frigate *Constitution* are at dock in the Charlestown Navy Yard at the turn of the century. The shaft of the Bunker Hill Monument can be seen towering above all on the left.

The Navy Yard was an extensive tract of land that fronted on the Mystic River. The Bunker Hill Monument rises from Breed's Hill in the rear of the Navy Yard in this turn-of-the-century photograph.

The frigate *Constitution*, before its restoration, is docked at the Navy Yard. With 87 acres, the Charlestown Navy Yard was among the busiest of the East Coast navy yards; after Charlestown was annexed to Boston in 1874, the yard was henceforth known as the Boston Navy Yard.

This panoramic view of the Navy Yard was taken from the top of the Lincoln Wharf Power House chimney.

Members of the crew of the *Atlanta* manned the yards while President Benjamin Harrison arrived aboard the *Baltimore* during the encampment of the Grand Army of the Republic, which was held in Boston in 1890. It was said that "men, masts, yards, and sails all join[ed] in a tableau of ceremonial anachronism"; this photograph attests to the excitement of the day.

In 1929, an aerial view of the Boston Navy Yard shows cruisers and ships at dock.

During the Great Depression, unemployed men would line up outside the Navy Yard in the hopes that some sort of job might be available.

The Sailors' Haven was at 46 Water Street in Charlestown near the gates of the Navy Yard. The former townhouse complex was used "as a reading-room for the seamen on board the ships moored in Charlestown. From its inception the men have crowded the place, and from a modest reading-room it has grown into a great institution. Today the whole brick building is in use; there are reading and writing rooms, billiards, games of all kinds, a large concert hall and a chapel."

A new Sailors' Haven was built in 1905 under the sponsorship of the Episcopal City Mission of Boston. With "accomodations for seamen at thirty five cents a night, including breakfast, the seamen could join in entertainment on Thursday evenings by the Ladies Aid and a carefully selected "Forward Watch Club" of young women ran regular dances and whist parties on certain other evenings." (Courtesy of the BPL.)

Six

City Square and the Training Field

Charlestown Town Hall was built in 1818 on the site of the old Robbins Tavern. Originally known as the Market House, the area was known as Market Square until 1847, when it was renamed "City Square." The town hall, an impressive neoclassical structure, was demolished in 1868 to make way for the new city hall. (Courtesy of the BPL.)

The Mansion House (on the left) and the Middlesex House were on the south side of City Square. The sidewalk encircling the fountain and garden of City Square can be seen on the right, and a horse-drawn omnibus is in the center of the street. (Courtesy of the BPL.)

Edward Everett (1794–1865) was one of Charlestown's most famous residents, living on Harvard Street in the 1830s. Born in Dorchester, he later became president of Harvard College, served in both the state and national legislatures, was governor of Massachusetts, and was ambassador to the Court of Saint James. Everett gave a two-hour oration at the dedication of the battlefield of the Battle of Gettysburg, though Abraham Lincoln's *"Four score and seven years ago . . ."* speech is far better remembered today.

Charles Devens (1820–1891) was attorney general in the cabinet of President Rutherford B. Hayes. It was he who suggested the president's first name when Charles River Avenue was being renamed, thereby perpetuating his name in Rutherford Avenue. A state senator, a U.S. Marshal, a major-general during the Civil War, and a justice of the Supreme Court, Devens was a well-respected son of Charlestown.

A triumphal arch was erected over Charles River Avenue for the Bunker Hill Day parade on June 17, 1876. An eagle surmounts the arch and the names "Warren" and "Putnam" grace either side. The Charlestown Neck streetcar passes underneath.

The Waverley House was an elegant building constructed in City Square in 1865. The facade extended along Warren Avenue to Front Street and housed a Millinery & Fancy Goods store, McLean's Boots & Shoes, and a Dry & Fancy Goods store, as well as Abbotsford Hall on the floor above. The cost for this impressive Second Empire block was nearly half a million dollars. (Courtesy of the BPL.)

Moses A. Dow (1810–1886) built the Waverley House in 1865 and it "was opened with great éclat, the city government of Charlestown being present and Mr. Dow being tendered a reception and banquet" following the festivities. Dow was the editor of the *Waverley Magazine*, which, although modest to start, eventually provided him with an ample fortune after it became a leading magazine in nineteenth-century America.

The Waverley House, on the right, was an impressive addition to City Square. On the left the street led to the Charlestown Bridge, which connected Charlestown to the North End of Boston.

Charlestown City Hall was an impressive French Second Empire structure that was designed by William Washburn and built on the site of the old town hall in Market Square.

During the early nineteenth century, a horse-drawn omnibus conveyed passengers from Charlestown across the bridge spanning the Charles River to points in Boston for a few cents each way.

After the street railways were replaced with trolleys, horses were no longer needed. These were among the last of the old railway horses that were used to pull carts in the early twentieth century.

The Charlestown Bridge spanned the Charles River connecting Charlestown and Boston. These two women walk toward Boston with the old city hall in the background. The Elevated Railway (or the "El" as it came to be known) can be seen on the right.

A number of Charlestown trolleys have stopped to allow a schooner to pass through the drawbridge spanning the Charles River between Boston and Charlestown. As numerous ships and schooners had to pass through these bridges to gain access to the harbor, traffic frequently backed up on both sides of the bridge.

By the turn of the twentieth century, the Charlestown Bridge was surmounted by the tracks of the Boston Elevated Railway's Dudley Station to Sullivan Station line. A thriving waterfront existed with numerous commercial concerns on piers projecting from both sides of the Charles River.

A view of City Square at the turn of the century shows the Elevated Railway passing through the square with a horse and carriage crossing the bridge. The former city hall was used for offices after Charlestown was annexed to Boston in 1874.

Tudor Wharf was the headquarters of Frederick Tudor, the "Ice King." Tudor created an export trade for cut ice from the ponds of Saugus. The blocks were coated in sawdust and shipped to warm climates where ice brought tremendous prices. Beginning in 1805, Tudor built up a thriving ice trade with the West Indies; his company eventually had to compete with other ice export companies such as Hittinger's, Gage & Company, and Damon's Ice Company.

The landing of the Warren Line, a transatlantic steamship line, was in Charlestown. The Warren Line serviced the Boston to Liverpool, England, route.

The Warren Line's building was on the site of the wharves of the former Hittinger's and Damon's Ice Companies. The Boston and Maine Railroad's Hoosic Tunnel docks were also located here; on the right is the White Star Liner *Canopic* at dock.

Damon's Wharf, once known as Harris Wharf, was owned by John W. Damon, a former partner of Frederick Tudor in the ice trade. Though both Damon and Tudor made their fortune in cut ice, they "had a falling out over business matters, and the two maintained an active feud for over twenty-five years."

The Elevated Railway approaches City Square in Charlestown from the bridge connecting the North End of Boston and Charlestown. As steel girders are erected to support the elevated rails, an overhead crane lays the supports to the tracks.

The Elevated Railway supports and railway bed are laid, and the rails are to be installed next in this c. 1900 photograph. On the left is Cowdrey's Candy Company and in the distance can be seen the twin spires of Saint Mary's Catholic Church in the North End of Boston.

A horse and cart pass under the Elevated Railway in this view looking toward the former city hall from Cowdrey's Candy Company. City Square Station was erected with a fanciful conductor's booth and was designed by Boston architect Alexander Wadsworth Longfellow in 1908; it was a side-platform station, different from the island station he designed in 1901 at Thompson Square. On the left is Rutherford Avenue.

City Square Station on the Elevated Railway had impressive details such as a conductor's booth, a waiting platform, and decorative railings. Literally cutting a swathe through City Square, the "El" cast a dark shadow on Charlestown for three quarters of a century, as the trains rumbled along Main Street from City Square to Sullivan Square.

By 1910, the City Square Station provided fast train service from Charlestown to Boston. However, streetcars still operated along the main streets for many years in addition to the "El."

The Elevated Railway crossed from Boston to Charlestown over the Charlestown Bridge. As the trains left North Station, a series of precarious turns would set the wheels of the train to squealing, creating an unique and special sound that was long associated with that part of town. Here horses, carriages, and carts pass under the "El" as a train crosses the bridge toward Charlestown.

Photographed in 1958 at City Square Station, a four-car train (a 1927 Laconia) is shown pulling into the station. These trains were replaced within a year with more modern cars that were part of the overall upgrading of the "Orange Line."

The Roughan Building was constructed in 1899 in City Square between Park and Main Streets. An impressive yellow brick commercial block with Romanesque Revival windows that arch toward the cornice, the building housed stores such as Griffin's (a haberdashery), the Charlestown Real Estate office, and a drug store on the first floor, with offices above. A large hall known as "Roughan's Hall," where dances were often held, was located on the top floor. Today, Olive's Restaurant is located on the first floor.

The Young Men's Christian Association (the Army and Navy YMCA) built a local branch in City Square, Charlestown, for the sailors whose ships were at dock in the Navy Yard. An impressive Classical Revival building of red brick and limestone detailing, its large arched windows encircled the building on the first floor.

The Army and Navy YMCA had a well-stocked reading room on the first floor where newspapers, periodicals, and a large selection of books were available. Here, a cozy alcove had club chairs and reading tables for those who enjoyed reading.

Winthrop Square was originally known as the Training Field. Named for Governor John Winthrop, the square was encircled with an impressive cast-iron fence and contained a monument to the soldiers and sailors from Charlestown who served during the Civil War.

The Soldiers' and Sailors' Monument was designed by Martin Milmore (1844–1883) and was dedicated on June 17, 1872. The monument "consists of a group of three figures, placed upon a lofty pedestal, the whole being thirty-three feet in height. The principal figure represents America in the act of crowning with laurel wreaths the symbol of the Army and the Navy, which are represented by two other figures, cut in the same material, the one a Soldier and the other a Sailor."

Seven
Craft's Corner or Thompson Square

Thompson Square is the intersection of Main, Harvard, Green, and Austin Streets and was named for Dr. Abraham Rand Thompson (1781–1866). Known as Craft's Corner in the early nineteenth century, it was enlarged in 1869 to its present configuration. In this photograph, looking toward Main and Harvard Streets, the Elevated Railway is being extended along Main Street at the turn of the century. On the left is the Charlestown Five Cent Savings Bank.

Elias Crafts' house, built by Mercy Hay Boylston, was probably the first to be built in Charlestown after the Battle of Bunker Hill. In the photograph, Charles V. Chase stands in front of the building he bought from the Crafts family in 1857. The building was demolished by order of the Charlestown City Council in 1869 to enlarge Thompson Square. (Courtesy of the BPL.)

Elias Crafts (1807–1899) opened a store at Crafts Corner, now known as Thompson Square, where he sold medicines and fancy goods. He was a popular man whose benevolent character was "known and liked by all physicians and is popular with young and old."

Thompson Square was named for Dr. Abraham Rand Thompson (1781–1866). It was said of this popular physician that "in his day he was one of the best known citizens of the commonwealth." A graduate of Dartmouth, where he received the degree of Doctor of Medicine, Thompson settled in Charlestown and "continued to practice [medicine] until the day of his death."

The Warren Tavern is at the corner of Warren Street and Monument Avenue. Built in 1780 and named in memory of Dr. Joseph Warren (1741–1775), it was among the first of the buildings constructed after the fire that destroyed Charlestown during the Revolution. Today, this colonial tavern still serves fine foods and libations in an authentic atmosphere.

Samuel Finley Breese Morse (1791–1872) was born in 1791 in this house on Main Street where his parents were staying until their own house in Charlestown was finished. A graduate of Yale (AB 1810, AM 1816) and an accomplished artist, Morse sent the first inter-city telegraph message in 1844 from the U.S. Supreme Court in Washington, DC, to Dr. Alfred Vail in Baltimore, MD. The message conveyed—in Morse code—was: "What had God wrought."

The Morse family was painted in 1811 by Samuel F.B. Morse in their Charlestown home. Reverend Jedediah Morse stands in the center discoursing on points of interest in the world; Reverend Morse is considered the father of American geography and was the first person to publish a text that specifically addressed that subject. From the left are Mrs. Jedediah Morse, Samuel F.B. Morse, Reverend Jedediah Morse, Richard Cary Morse, and Sidney Edwards Morse. (Courtesy of the Smithsonian Institution, National Museum of History and Technology.)

The William Hurd House was at the corner of Main Street and Hurd's Lane. Built in 1785, it was an impressive three-story mansion built on land confiscated from Thomas Fletcher, a loyalist who fled America during the Revolution. The house was later demolished in 1888. (Courtesy of the BPL.)

The Richard Frothingham House stood at 2 Eden Street with the facade facing Main Street. Richard Frothingham, the noted historian, stands beside the gate; two women are seated beside him. The house was demolished in the early 1960s. (Courtesy of the BPL.)

The Dexter-Bridge-Davidson-Lockwood House was built on Green Street (facing Main Street) by the Honorable Samuel Dexter Jr. An impressive Federal mansion with a spacious garden bounded by Main and High Streets, it was one of Charlestown's most impressive properties in the nineteenth century. Today, it still stands next to the First Church in Charlestown, having been purchased from the Lockwood family by the Abraham Lincoln Post 11, Grand Army of the Republic. (Courtesy of Roger Greene and Marion Diener.)

Samuel Dexter Jr. was a member of the U.S. Senate when he resigned in 1800 to become secretary of war under President John Adams. He later served as secretary of the treasury, continuing under President Thomas Jefferson. As minister to Spain under President James Madison, he served the United States with great éclat.

Rhodes Greene Lockwood (1807–1872) married Sally Maria Davidson, the daughter of Hamilton Davidson of Charlestown. They made their home in her father's house and greatly improved the horticultural gardens. (Courtesy of Roger Greene and Marion Diener.)

The Lockwood Mansion was photographed in the 1870s with a granite retaining wall and cast-iron fences encircling the gardens. (Courtesy of Roger Greene and Marion Diener.)

The Kettell House was at the junction of Chestnut and Adams Streets. Built in 1790 by Thomas Russell, it was originally the Russell Academy of Charlestown. In 1810, it became a duplex house occupied by the Dana and Russell families and remained as such until it was purchased by Nathan Adams, for whom Adams Street was named. Adams' daughter was Mrs. George A. Kettell. (Courtesy of the BPL.)

A "tramp resting under tree" was photographed at the turn of the century outside the Kettell House at Adams and Chestnut Streets. With a shady tree, and an obviously sun-dappled afternoon, who could resist such a temptation? (Courtesy of the BPL.)

Colonel Laommi Baldwin, an engineer credited with the success of the Middlesex Canal, lived in this house on Main Street. It was said by Professor Vose of the Massachusetts Institute of Technology that "no man so well deserves the name of Father of Civil Engineering in America as Laommi Baldwin . . . there were very few works of internal improvement carried out in America during the first thirty years of the present century [the nineteenth] which Mr. Baldwin was not connected." (Courtesy of the BPL.)

The home of Dr. H.A. Houghton was at 12 Cordis Street. Built by Charles Thompson, a state senator and moderator at town meetings for many years, the house had a garden that extended to Warren Street and had both Chinese wisteria and buckthorn hedges. (Courtesy of the BPL.)

Along Main Street were numerous commercial concerns in early nineteenth-century houses. The thriving businesses included, from left to right: the New York Butter & Grocery House, the M.J. Enwright Gilding and Picture Frame Company (with Dr. Roy's office above), and Allbe's Printing Office. (Courtesy of Bill Nolan.)

Main Street at the corner of Monument Avenue has an impressive late eighteenth-century mansion that has had storefronts on the first floor for over a century. A woman looks at the display in the window of Twomey's Bargain Store, and on the left is J.W. Rand, who sold hats, trunks, furs, and furnishing goods. On the far left can be seen the townhouses rising on Monument Avenue. (Courtesy of Bill Nolan.)

The Elevated Railway is progressing along Main Street at the turn of the century. A young man steps off the sidewalk opposite Horan's Furniture Emporium, which was at the corner of Main and Union Streets. (Courtesy of the BPL.)

Firemen ascend ladders mounted against houses on Monument Avenue between Main and Warren Streets. The steep rise of Monument Avenue, with the sleek shaft of the Bunker Hill Monument crowning the top of Breed's Hill, can be seen in the background. (Courtesy of Bill Nolan.)

The Charlestown Five Cents Savings Bank was incorporated in 1854 and was "one of the representative and reliable savings institutions in Boston." Its headquarters were in an elaborate Gothic Revival building in Thompson Square, which is today a Boston landmark.

The Warren Institution for Savings was incorporated in 1829 with Timothy Walker serving as the first president. It was said at the turn of the century that the "Warren Institution for Savings has a reputation for soundness and able management that is not confined to the limits of Charlestown, but extends throughout the commonwealth."

The Bunker Hill
National Bank was
bedecked with flags and
bunting when it was
photographed on June
17, 1875. Incorporated
in 1825, the bank was
in City Square,
formerly Market
Square, at the
northwest corner of
Park Street. (Courtesy
of the BPL.)

The interior of the
Bunker Hill National
Bank had impressive
oak woodwork with
teller cages of
intricately wrought
metal. Note the
spittoon on the floor.

Main Street in Thompson Square, photographed in the 1960s, had become overcast by the shadow of the Elevated Railway. Though the pier supports were on the edges of the streets, the darkness caused by the elevated tracks cast a somber view for seven decades. (Courtesy of James F. O'Brien.)

These soldiers pose on a horse-drawn wagon on Main Street after the end of World War II. The Thompson Square Theatre is on the far left. (Courtesy of James F. O'Brien.)

The Massachusetts State Prison was in Charlestown at Prison Point, the present site of the Bunker Hill Community College on Austin Street. Originally built by Charles Bulfinch, the prison was greatly enlarged by Gridley J. Fox Bryant in the mid-nineteenth century. Here, the warden's house was in front of the octagonal pavilion of the granite prison. (Courtesy of the BPL.)

Gideon Haynes (1815–1892) was appointed warden of the Massachusetts State Prison by Governor Nathaniel P. Banks. A former state senator, Haynes was an efficient organizer. One source remarked that at the time the prison was "in a state of chaos but Mr. Haynes by skill and patience soon righted matters, and when he ceased to be warden it was a model working prison."

The chain shop at the Massachusetts State Prison was a large shop where chain links of different sizes were manufactured for use in the prison, in the Navy Yard for anchors, or in local manufactories. These furnaces would be fired six days a week and prisoners would be required to produce chains, link by link, for their keep.

The officials of the Massachusetts State Prison established classrooms where many of the prisoners could learn to read and write. Here, prisoners are in a geography class with multicolored maps of the United States affixed to the poles supporting the ceiling.

Eight
Bunker Hill and Monument Square

The Bunker Hill Monument was etched in an 1848 view entitled *Perspective View of Bunker Hill Monument*. The shaft of the monument rises from Breed's Hill, where the Battle of Bunker Hill took place in 1775. The cornerstone of the monument was laid on June 17, 1825, following an oration by the Honorable Daniel Webster. By the 1840s, the area had been laid out as Monument Square with substantial townhouses facing the park. (Courtesy of Roger Greene and Marion Diener.)

Looking up Monument Avenue on June 17, 1875, bunting and flags adorn the townhouses for the celebration of Bunker Hill Day. (Courtesy of James F. O'Brien.)

At the top of Monument Avenue as it intersects Monument Square, the shaft of the Bunker Hill Monument looms 225 feet tall, far above the rooftops of the houses on either side. (Courtesy of James F. O'Brien.)

The *Firemens' Quick Step* was performed on September 10, 1840, when it was composed by George Hews and dedicated to the Bunker-Hill Whig Convention that was held that year. In this fanciful print that adorned the flyleaf of the sheet music, the unfinished Bunker Hill Monument has a flag waiving in the wind from the top of the shaft while cavaliers and soldiers march to the music of the Quick Step.

Eliza Henderson Boardman Otis was the second wife of Mayor Otis of Boston. A vain and feckle society lady, she proposed to sell kisses at $5 each during the week-long festival held at Fanueil Hall in 1842 to raise the funds to complete the Bunker Hill Monument. One wonders how many gentlemen availed themselves of this rare chance to assist Mrs. Otis in raising the funds to complete the monument! (Courtesy of the Gibson House Museum.)

The Bunker Hill Monument has 90 courses of granite. The stone was quarried in Quincy by Solomon Willard, an engineer who was "projector and engineer of the Granite Railway . . . the inventor of the eight wheel car, the portable derrick and many other important improvements in railway machinery and equipment." The base of the monument is 30 feet square, and 15 feet at the top. To ascend to the observatory in the top, one ascends 294 stairs. On the left is the Charlestown High School, built in 1870.

The interior of the observation booth at the top of the Bunker Hill Monument has spectacular vistas in all directions. This print from 1876, which was sketched by Joseph Becker, shows an elderly lady reaching the top steps as others enjoy the view. (Courtesy of the BPL.)

Two riders sit astride their horses on Chestnut Street at the turn of the century.

Charlestown, Mass. Bunker Hill Monument from Chestnut Street.

Looking toward Concord Street, the townhouses along Monument Avenue effect an impressive streetscape by the 1880s. Designed by Solomon Willard and built by James Savage, the Bunker Hill Monument was an engineering feat that brought visitors from far and wide to see the scene of the battle and revel in the fact that the "views from the top of the monument are justly considered among the finest in the world." (Courtesy of James F. O'Brien.)

105

A mother strolls past the Bunker Hill Monument with a perambulator opposite the block of Monument Square between Pleasant Street and Monument Avenue in the 1890s.

Looking from the corner of Tremont Street and Monument Square, the Bunker Hill Monument was between the dome of the First Congregational Church and the Trinity Methodist Church. On the right of the monument is King Solomon's Lodge of Masons.

The statue of Colonel William Prescott was sculpted by William W. Story, portraying the patriot who led his troops up Breed's Hill dressed in a broad-brimmed hat and a banyan jacket. It was Prescott who shouted, "Don't fire 'till you see the whites of their eyes!"

John Morrison and his shadow stand in front of the plinth base of the Prescott statue in 1940.

This building at 7 Monument Square and its connected neighbors created an urban streetscape of red brick townhouses. With swell bay facades and uniform roof lines, some with cupolas, the area of Monument Square became an elegant neighborhood by the mid-nineteenth century. (Courtesy of the BPL.)

The Stone Mansion was built at the corner of Bartlett and Concord Streets in the 1840s. A duplex Greek Revival house, the side facing Bartlett Street had four monumental Ionic columns supporting a pedimented dormer. Mayor Phineas Jones Stone stands in the garden while family members pose on the second-floor porch and the side of the porch on Concord Street. (Courtesy of John and Betty Walsh.)

High Street, looking toward 1 and 2 Monument Square, is seen in the 1870s from Cross Street. These flat-facade townhouses with their projecting steps made for an interesting view of mid-nineteenth-century development in Charlestown. (Courtesy of the BPL.)

The Austin-Dillon House is at the corner of High and Wood Streets. A substantial Italianate mansion with a mansard roof, it was built by the Austin family next to the Trinity Methodist Church. The house was later owned by Francis H. Dillon, who was described as "one of the most prominent and substantial citizens and business men of this progressive district" at the turn of the century. (Courtesy of Barbara Acton and Ursula Patterson.)

Active in local affairs, Francis H. Dillon served as a representative for Charlestown, where it was said that "his aid has been invaluable, though of the kind that does not proclaim itself by means of a brass band." (Courtesy of Francis H. Dillon.)

The Dillon family posed for this family portrait in the garden of their house on High Street in 1903. From left to right are: (front row) Helen Dillon (holding Gertrude A. Dillon), Deliah Mary Dillon (Mrs. Francis H., holding Louise Dillon), Emily N. Dillon, Francis H. Dillon, Mae Dillon, and William Dillon; (back row) an unidentified maid, Alice Dillon, and Francis H. Dillon Jr. (Courtesy of William Dillon Blake.)

Nine

From Bunker Hill Street
to Sullivan Square

The view toward the
north from the Bunker
Hill Monument shows
the area of the Mystic
River and Chelsea,
Massachusetts. In the
foreground are some of
the many streets
between Monument
Avenue and Medford
Street. (Courtesy of
James F. O'Brien.)

Oliver Holden (1765–1844) was the son of Nehemiah and Elizabeth Mitchell Holden. A well-known composer who published *The Union Harmony or Universal Collection of Sacred Music*, he was best known for his hymn *Coronation*. These lines from the hymn were engraved upon his tomb in the Phipps Street Burial Ground: "All hail the power of Jesus' name, Let Angels prostrate fall; Bring forth the royal diadem, And crown him Lord of all."

The Holden House was on Pearl Street at the corner of Bunker Hill Street. An impressive house known as the "elegant reserve," it later became the home of Thomas Doane, engineer of the Hoosic Tunnel and founder of Doane College in Crete, Nebraska. The Oliver Holden School was later built on the site. (Courtesy of the BPL.)

Alson Studley (1794–1871) "came to Charlestown in 1826, and established the first stage line between Boston and Charlestown, the first trip being made June 17. The Saturday Evening Gazette of June 26, 1826, said, 'An hourly stage has been established to run hourly from City Tavern (Brattle Street) to Richardson Tavern on Charlestown Neck (Sullivan Square) . . . Fare 12 1/2 cents.' "

A parade approaches Sullivan Square on Bunker Hill Day, June 17, 1946, from Bunker Hill Street. The parade was photographed from the Elevated Railway, whose tracks can be seen on the right. (Courtesy of the BPL.)

Sullivan Square was named for Governor James Sullivan (1744–1808), the fifth governor of the Commonwealth. At various point in his life, Sullivan served Massachusetts and the nation as a member of the superior court, state legislature, and Continental Congress, as well as the being the president of the Middlesex Canal (1793–1808) and the attorney general of Massachusetts (1790–1807). Sullivan Square was an attractive park located on the former Charlestown Neck, with a circular area surrounded by a cast-iron fence. A fountain graced the center of the charming square, which was later swept away by the Elevated Railway at the turn of the century.

Bunker Hill Street, seen looking south from Elm Street at the turn of the century, had a number of corner stores. A streetcar approaches from Sullivan Square.

This trolley obviously wasn't making stops when it was photographed on Bunker Hill Street in the late 1940s.

Sullivan Square Station was the terminus of the Elevated Railway that connected Roxbury and Charlestown. Sullivan Square was built in 1901 as a huge terminus station for both the Elevated line and the streetcars that connected the station to outlying communities such as Somerville and Medford. A waiting room, spaces for billiards, and retail space occupied the ground level, and the main level allowed for access to the trains. A mezzanine contained the offices of the Elevated Railway Company.

The front of the Sullivan Square Terminal was an impressive red brick structure that commanded attention from all vantage points. The distance between Roxbury and Charlestown was 5 miles, and the Elevated Railway could run this line in twenty-two minutes, far more quickly than the streetcars.

The interior of the Sullivan Square Terminal had a platform on the right where passengers coming from Boston would exit the cars. On the far left are the streetcars that would pick up and discharge passengers arriving at the station.

The rear of the Sullivan Square Terminal had an arched wall of glass. The interior was 62 feet high with eleven iron arches spanning 175 feet. The Elevated Railway cars on the left would turn around to return on the route to Boston and the streetcars in the foreground would connect Somerville and Medford to the station.

These employees were being honored in 1928 for fifty years or more service to the Elevated Railway. From left to right are: (front row) Patrick Roach, James Kenney, A.L. Hauser, John Howard, Patrick Horan, William Pett, James Smith, Timothy Connell, Andrew Blake, Henry Bryant, Patrick Kelly, George Clark, and John Sullivan; (back row) F.E. Hanington, C.H. Lewis, Robert Nelson, Patrick Donoghue, Richard Moore, T. Devine, Frank Holbrook, John Carl, C.I. Chadbourne, Frank Brown, Charles Seaver, George Costello, Austin Shuttleworth, and George Gilman.

A group of employees of the Elevated Railway pose for their graduation photograph from the educational program of the Instruction School of the Elevated Railway for the year 1927–28. Edward Dane, in the center of the first row, was general manager of the Boston Elevated Railway and urged the employees to avail themselves of the school, which was located in Sullivan Square.

Ten
Industrial
Charlestown

Nason's Fruit and Provision Store was at the corner of Bartlett and Green Streets. Mr. Nason (on the left) and a clerk stand in front of the shop, a typical corner grocery store of the late nineteenth century. George Nason, son of the owner, and his friend Albert Briggs sit on the seat of the delivery wagon for orders that were dispatched throughout Charlestown. (Courtesy of the BPL.)

Hamilton Davidson was in business as a wholesale grain merchant on the Boston wharf known as the Baltimore Packet Pier on Commercial Street. Davidson had purchased the property of the Middlesex Canal Company in the area of Charlestown Neck, which was later the site of the Davidson Syringe Company. (Courtesy of Roger Greene and Marion Diener.)

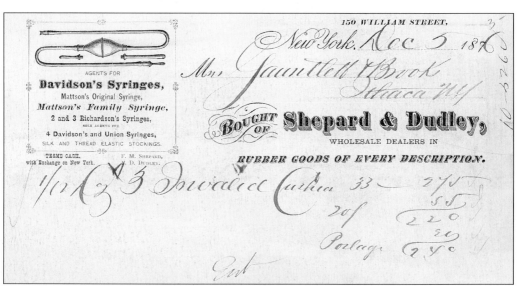

The Davidson Syringe was patented by Rhodes Greene Lockwood and was a rubber device that consisted of a tube with a rubber bulb that could draw fluids, ejecting them in a stream. The company made rubber goods of every description, and was a prominent manufacturer "of the finest grades of rubber goods used in medicine, surgery, stationery, and fine work, and their productions go to all parts of the world."

Rufus Barrus Stickney (1824–1891) was president of the Stickney and Poor Spice Company. Founded in 1815, the spice business started in a small way when Stickney's father "began to prepare mustard for the table, grinding it by hand, carrying his product to his customers in a hand basket." Rufus Stickney, in association with John R. Poor, opened a spice mill in Charlestown in 1850, where the two men became the "largest grinders of pure spices in the world."

The factory of the Stickney and Poor Spice Company was at the corner of Cambridge and Spice Streets. Built in 1867 of red brick with a mansard roof, the factory became a leading manufacturer of spices, and winner of two gold medals, in 1890 and 1892, for the "purity and quality" of prepared spices, extracts, and mustards.

Ezekiel Byam was the "pioneer of match manufacturers." His father had made lucifer matches as early as the 1830s, but it was Ezekiel Byam who was "the first to obtain a right for the manufacture of the American friction matches." His firm, the Diamond Match Company, made wood matches inexpensively, at a cost of a 1¢ for 300 matches. Previously, a "bunch" of 104 matches cost a 25¢.

Alonzo Van Nostrand originated the "P.B." trademark for his ale that was brewed in Charlestown in the late nineteenth century. His Bunker Hill Brewery bottled ale in the English fashion to compete with Bass, but "P.B." ale had "a reputation second to none in the Commonwealth, and is the only malt liquor used in the Massachusetts General and the Boston City hospitals and other institutions for the sick and convalescent." Many citizens of the Commonwealth—not only the convalescent—enjoyed Van Nostrand's brew.

W.F. Schrafft and Sons was at the corner of Causeway and Charlestown Streets before it was moved to Sullivan Square. As a manufacturer of confectioneries and bonbons, Schrafft's became a leading name in nationwide candy sales in the twentieth century.

William F. Schrafft was the founder of Schrafft's Candy Company. His sons, George and William Schrafft, continued the family business in Sullivan Square in Charlestown, where their Art Deco factory had a prominent clock that could be seen from all directions, as well as an illuminated sign that proclaimed their name.

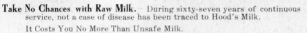

YOUR CHILDREN NEED HOOD'S MILK

HOOD'S MILK IS PERFECTLY PASTEURIZED

Because over 5,000 people have been made sick in Boston in the last few years from using raw, unsafe milk.

HOOD'S MILK IS PERFECTLY PASTEURIZED

Because the best health authorities in the world say that this prevents children from getting tuberculosis, typhoid fever, scarlet fever, diphtheria and sore throat from milk.

Take No Chances with Raw Milk. During sixty-seven years of continuous service, not a case of disease has been traced to Hood's Milk.
It Costs You No More Than Unsafe Milk.

H. P. Hood & Sons

Hood Milk, until recently located on Rutherford Avenue, had a series of advertisements at the turn of the century that stressed the fact that children not only enjoyed, but required, Hood's Milk. It was said that during "sixty-seven years of continuous service, not a case of disease has been traced to Hood's Milk."

Harvey P. Hood founded his milk empire in Derry, New Hampshire. He collected milk from dairy farms in the area, and shipped it to Boston dealers daily. When he learned that the raw milk could transmit disease, however, Hood began the pasteurization of milk. This process practically eliminated the threat of tuberculosis, typhoid fever, scarlet fever, and diphtheria from unprocessed milk.

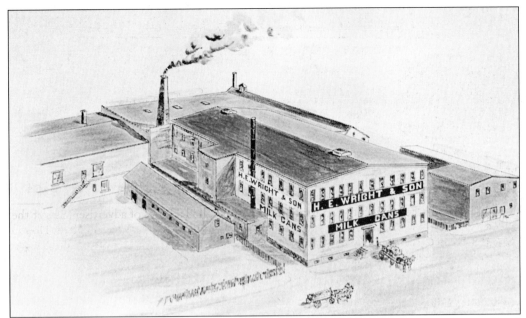

The factory of Henry E. Wright and Son was on Spice Street, where milk cans were produced for the numerous dairy farms sending milk to Boston.

E.T. Cowdrey Company produced jellies, preserves, canned goods, pickles, and sauces in their factory on Charles River (later Rutherford) Avenue in City Square.

J.O. Chase and Company was a hack, boarding, and livery stable at 60 Lawrence Street. In the nineteenth century, hacks were horse-drawn cabs that could be hired to get from one place to another. Livery stables arose in larger cities and towns as places where horses and carriages could be hired with a driver for the day, and also where one's horse could be boarded. A top-hatted driver sits on the seat of a fashionable carriage in 1895 outside the stable's entrance.

The carriages and wagons available at the turn of the century ran the gamut from broughams, rockaways, surreys, buggies, and sleighs to depot wagons, breaks, and carts.

The Charlestown Gas Light Company had an annual output of a hundred million "feet" of gas at the turn of the century. By the late nineteenth century, the company provided all of Charlestown and Somerville and a part of Medford with gas and electricity. Located on Arlington Avenue near Sullivan Square, the plant consisted of two gas holders, a retort house, a purifying house, and an electrical plant.

The Boston Bakery of the United States Baking Company was located at 465 Medford Street, on the banks of the Mystic River.

Acknowledgments

I would like to thank the following persons for their continued support and encouragement in the writing of this book on Charlestown, Massachusetts. This book is one of a series on the neighborhoods of the City of Boston; without the interest and assistance of the following people, and in many cases the loaning of family photographs, these books would lack much of their appeal:

Barbara Acton; Daniel J. Ahlin; William Dillon Blake; Anthony Bognanno; Paul and Helen Graham Buchanan; Mary Jo Campbell; Lorna Condon of the Society for the Preservation of New England Antiquities; Gloria Conway, editor of the *Charlestown Patriot*; Dexter; Francis H. Dillon; Reverend Victor Ford of the First Parish Church in Charlestown; Edward W. Gordon, whose architectural survey of Charlestown prepared for the Boston Landmarks Commission was of great assistance; Roger Greene and Marion Diener; Virginia Holbrook; James Z. Kyprianos; Lesley C. Loke; Maureen S. Marx, Branch Librarian, and Theresa Francisco of the Charlestown Branch, Boston Public Library; the late Misses Mary and Jennie Mitchell; William Nolan; James F. O'Brien; Stephen and Susan Paine; Reverend Michael Parise; Ursula Patterson; William H. Pear; Dennis Ryan; Anthony and Mary Mitchell Sammarco; Rosemary Sammarco; Sylvia Sandeen; Joyce Stevens of Heritage Education; William Varrell; Arthur Walsh; John J. and Betty Walsh; and Sue Warner of the Yale University Art Gallery.